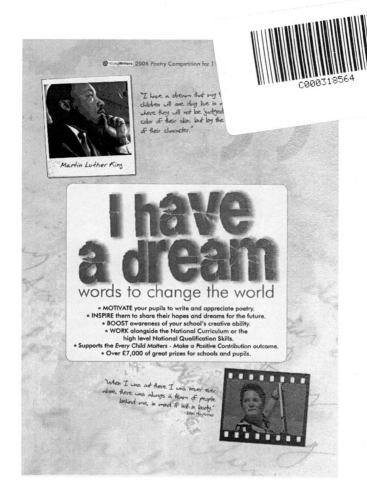

YoungWriters 2006 Poetry Competition for 1

"I have a dream that my f
children will one day live in a
where they will not be judged
color of their skin, but by the
of their character."

Martin Luther King

I have a dream
words to change the world

- MOTIVATE your pupils to write and appreciate poetry.
- INSPIRE them to share their hopes and dreams for the future.
- BOOST awareness of your school's creative ability.
- WORK alongside the National Curriculum or the
  high level National Qualification Skills.
- Supports the Every Child Matters - Make a Positive Contribution outcome.
- Over £7,000 of great prizes for schools and pupils.

"When I was at there I was never ever
alone, there was always a team of people
behind me, in mind if not in body."
- Ellen MacArthur

Wales Vol I
Edited by Lynsey Hawkins

 Young**Writers**

First published in Great Britain in 2006 by:
Young Writers
Remus House
Coltsfoot Drive
Peterborough
PE2 9JX
Telephone: 01733 890066
Website: www.youngwriters.co.uk

SB ISBN 1 84602 533 8

Foreword

Imagine a teenager's brain; a fertile yet fragile expanse teeming with ideas, aspirations, questions and emotions. Imagine a classroom full of racing minds, scratching pens writing an endless stream of ideas and thoughts . . .

. . . Imagine your words in print reaching a wider audience. Imagine that maybe, just maybe, your words can make a difference. Strike a chord. Touch a life. Change the world. Imagine no more . . .

'I Have a Dream' is a series of poetry collections written by 11 to 18-year-olds from schools and colleges across the UK and overseas. Pupils were invited to send us their poems using the theme 'I Have a Dream'. Selected entries range from dreams they've experienced to childhood fantasies of stardom and wealth, through inspirational poems of their dreams for a better future and of people who have influenced and inspired their lives.

The series is a snapshot of who and what inspires, influences and enthuses young adults of today. It shows an insight into their hopes, dreams and aspirations of the future and displays how their dreams are an escape from the pressures of today's modern life. Young Writers are proud to present this anthology, which is truly inspired and sure to be an inspiration to all who read it.

Contents

Pen-Y-Dre High School, Merthyr Tydfil

The Poems

I Have A Dream

Believe
Dreams can come true
Try
To reach your full potential
Be
Who you were born to be
Dream
The world a better place
Think
If what you're doing is right
Feel proud of your world
Change
The good for the better
Inspire
You are one hand in one nation
Imagine
You could be that one . . .

Ben Callow (12)
Barry Comprehensive School, Barry

My Dream Poem

I have a dream
To see racism end
I have a dream
To make a difference
I have a dream
To see poverty end
I have a dream
For everyone to get along
I have a dream
To influence the next generation
I have a dream
For no more wars
I have a dream
For peace in the world.

Michael Harvey (11)
Barry Comprehensive School, Barry

Imagine

Imagine
The world was perfect
Imagine
It was calm
Imagine
There were no wars
Imagine
Everyone loved each other
Imagine
Families reunited
Imagine
No one was poor
Imagine
Finding the cure for cancer
Imagine
Everyone getting along
Imagine
No racism
Imagine
Just imagine it.

Jake Haysham (14)
Barry Comprehensive School, Barry

Status Symbols On Every Seam

('You have a much better life if you wear impressive clothes'. Vivienne Westwood)

The fourth bodily function: dressing
Touching everyone in its orbit
Designers emblazoning names across nubile anatomies
Turning fabric into the purest form of art,
Designing for optimum visual effect
Conceptually, aesthetically developing
Tangible forms of spiritual uplift,
A new kind of designer deliverance
Skills that require time, talent and a steady hand
Blending sexuality and outrageous behaviour,
A business brain in the frame
Continuing to make fashion exciting
Seductive colours; lavish surface textures,
Fashion: not about the clothes
But the people.

Lauren Cattle (18)
Barry Comprehensive School, Barry

I Have A Dream

Imagine
You had loads of money to give to homeless people
Imagine
You could stop all wars around the world like Iraq
Imagine
There was enough food for everyone round the world
Imagine
We had enough medicine to cure all diseases and cancers
Imagine
Racist people realised we are all the same inside
Imagine
There was less debt and less poor countries in the world
Imagine
Bullies knew the affect on their victims' lives
Imagine
The world was a better place to live in.

Rhys Kerslake (14)
Barry Comprehensive School, Barry

Ronan O'Gara

Ronan O'Gara
Try scorer
Conversion kicker
Fast runner

Ronan O'Gara
The hero
Helps his team win
Just like speedway

Ronan O'Gara
Rugby pitch hero
Whizzing star
Like a rocket

Ronan O'Gara
Singing loud and clear
Scoring try after try
Conversion after conversion.

Ryan McPeake (11)
Barry Comprehensive School, Barry

Changes

Consider having a better life,
Trying to help the ones in need,
Trying to make a worldwide change,
A positive change.

You run then leap for the chance and you succeed,
The chance that you would give your life for has come at last,
You guard this chance with your life,
You don't let it go or slip out of your hand.

The amazing chance that would go worldwide
And people will follow in your footsteps
And the fame and joy of changing other's lives for life,
People will make changes to their children's lives
And so it will carry on in the generations.

Sion Sutton (11)
Barry Comprehensive School, Barry

My Dream

There's a man who I look up to, he's my friend
Sometimes my enemy and my coach

He helps me train hard, on my bike, in the gym
That's why I like him

He believes in me and has taken a chance
We travel far, America, Belgium, Holland and France

This man has taken me from the tiny bikes to the shiny ones
Slow ones to fast ones

He's been into motocross since a boy
These machines are certainly not toys

He has taught me to jump so that my helmet can touch the sky
My love for motocross will never *die!*

Callum Sloman (12)
Barry Comprehensive School, Barry

Who's Your Inspiration?

We all have inspirations,
Whether it's sporting,
Someone close to you
Or someone who perceives.

There's always Jamie Oliver,
Or even Martin Luther King,
Who both stood up for what they thought was right.

You could also have a closer inspiration,
Whether it's family or a friend,
Think what they went through
And if it's anything you would do.

Then there's me
My one is Gareth Thomas,
He's gone through hard times
But he's still stuck by it.

So just think, you could make a difference
To how the world is run,
So be like Martin Luther King and keep on going,
The most important thing is,
Don't give up!

Luke O'Sullivan (12)
Barry Comprehensive School, Barry

I Have A Dream . . .

I have a dream with things
That could change my life,
Swords that are really pencils.

Actions appear more than words,
Standing up to your friends,
Is more important than treating them wrongly.

Treat things right all the time,
Stand up to your enemies, it is not bad,
Just try and then it will work.

Things will change and happen
That is life
And it will never, ever change.

Birds are mightier than planes,
Whoosh! as they go by
Things get hard,
Some people give up.

Dreams happen often
And it feels like they come true,
Never, never, never give up!

Lewis Cummings (12)
Barry Comprehensive School, Barry

I Have A Dream

I have a dream
That everybody will be equal
I have a dream
That peace will spread
Throughout the world

I have a dream
That everyone will be free men
I have a dream
That pollution will be
A thing of the past

I have a dream
That reading will influence the world
I have a dream
That every person's dream
Can be fulfilled.

Alex Champ (12)
Barry Comprehensive School, Barry

The Equal World

I have a dream today that every living human being shall be
Equal, no matter what his or her skin colour consists of,
No matter how much richer or poorer they might be.
I have a dream that the world shall be a place
Of peace, that the words 'fighting' and
'War' shall be kicked out of the
English dictionary.
I have a dream that
All countries shall come
Together and reunite as a whole.
I have a dream that women, men, black
People and white people shall be seen as the same
Person, that no person should differ from one another. I
Have a dream that the world be an equal place for all our sakes.

Alex Grigoriou (14)
Barry Comprehensive School, Barry

Why Can't We Learn?

Why can't we learn?
Learn that nobody is the same,
Everyone has a name,
A name that should be known.

I dream that one day,
Everybody can become one,
What do you dream?
Do you dream the same?

Why can't we learn?
Learn never to judge a book by its cover
But by what it contains
No matter its size or shape.

We all have our cultures,
Whether it's headbanging to your favourite band,
Or watching the footie with all your friends,
It's your culture.

What haven't we learnt?
But to learn more about each other
And how each other's cultures are
And how they work.

My culture is going out with my friends
And being proud that I am Welsh,
There is more to people than just their culture,
Everyone is different, it takes just a little time to learn this,
So why should we moan and groan all the time,
When we can just learn?

Thomas Richards (15)
Barry Comprehensive School, Barry

I Have A Dream

Imagine
Being on the professional pitch
Imagine
Scoring a classic goal
Imagine
Playing with professional players
Imagine
The whole world knowing your name
Imagine
Going on tour and meeting new players
Imagine
Playing in a stadium and everyone shouting your name
Imagine
Having your face printed all over the world
Imagine
Just being there
Imagine
It, can you just imagine it?

Rhys West (13)
Barry Comprehensive School, Barry

All The Dreams

Things can be dreams
Leading
To things you like
Leading
Others to victory
Leading
To your hopes and dreams
Leading
Other people
Leading
And inspiring people by
Leading
From dreams to success
Leading
By defending.

Jacob Adams (11)
Barry Comprehensive School, Barry

Captive

It's night, it's day,
But here I will stay,
All my brothers and sisters,
Have been taken away.

The sounds of screaming,
The smell of the blood,
I stand dreaming,
Then fall with a thud.

The noise of the soldiers,
Marching on by,
Fills me with sadness,
As I begin to cry.

Alone and forgotten,
The birds begin to sing,
The hopes and joys that
Freedom may bring.

It is only a dream,
'Tis nothing more,
An escape from reality,
To the ones I adore.

But hope is forever,
It never gives in,
It is what keeps us going,
From the heart, from within.

Elliot Hanson (14)
Barry Comprehensive School, Barry

I Have A Dream

Seeing these pictures,
Feeling the impact,
I try to feel what they are,
It's impossible.

Soon I will see this disaster,
I'm getting on a plane,
Far, far away,
I'm going for help.

I'm strolling the streets,
If you can call them that,
Homeless people sitting in the drought
Feeling lonely, hungry and thirsty.

Walking through villages,
Seeing starving people,
Babies crying through malnutrition,
I want to help.

I hand out food to needy people,
I help people and talk to them,
They cope as best they can,
I'm glad I'm helping these people.

And you know what?
It's making me feel great.

Amy Winter (13)
Cyfarthfa High School, Merthyr Tydfil

I Had A Dream

I had a dream:
The world was calm;
No fighting,
No shooting,
No firearms,
No warfare,
No famine,
No poverty.
When we love one another
And we're kind to all,
Children sleep safe at night:
That's what makes the world right.

Callum Palmer (12)
Cyfarthfa High School, Merthyr Tydfil

I Have A Dream

I dream of leaving Africa,
The poverty left behind,
To live in a better land,
Of a country full of wealth and hope.

Will this land fulfil my dream?
A comfortable bed, a belly full,
Clean fresh water that will be on tap,
Soft warm clothes upon my back.

Will this land of wealth and hope,
Give me freedom to roam
And the sun on my back?
Will I miss the sunset on the plain
Or is Africa the place of my dreams?

Daniel Williams (11)
Cyfarthfa High School, Merthyr Tydfil

I Have A Dream

I have a dream of a world
A world that's full of happiness
That's rid of poverty

I have a dream of a world
A world without any wars
Where everyone works together

I have a dream of a world
A world with no suffering
With no pain and sadness

I have a dream of a world
A world that will stop and think
A world that can forgive and forget

I have a dream
That this world was better
That this dream was a reality.

Lewes Phillips (12)
Cyfarthfa High School, Merthyr Tydfil

World Peace

A peaceful world,
Free of corruption,
Free of pollution,
Avoiding destruction.

A contented world,
Comfortable with life,
Comfortable with one another,
Accepting all race and colour.

A pleasant world,
With independence and curiosity,
With good intentions
And innocence rather than guilt.

A creative world,
Full of imagination,
Full of generosity,
The absence of cruelty.

An advanced world,
Gifted with technology,
Gifted with intelligence,
But not here to take advantage of.

A peaceful world,
Free of corruption,
Free of pollution,
Succeeding in all aspects of what a peaceful world should include.

Rebecca Mummery (13)
Cyfarthfa High School, Merthyr Tydfil

I Have A Dream

Just close my eyes - another daze,
The time passes me by.
Thoughts of the world and the people in it,
Are they laughing or do they cry?

Screams and shouts, in anger and pain,
Drown out all the sorrow.
More dry seasons, all year round
And another year to follow.

I have a dream to change all this,
To stop all war and hate.
I have a dream to change the world,
Before it becomes too late.

Rhian Fuller (13)
Cyfarthfa High School, Merthyr Tydfil

I Have A Dream

Wouldn't it be good if:
Everyone in the world would never go hungry,
Never went thirsty,
Never slept without shelter,
Never lived in fear,
Never started war,
Never died before the promised age,
Never lived under oppression,
Never polluted the planet,
Or hunted animals to extinction,
This is my dream,
If only it was so.

Jack William Morgan (11)
Cyfarthfa High School, Merthyr Tydfil

I Have A Dream

Water, water it should be free,
A gift from God for all to see.
But problems it causes to many a land,
So somebody should make a stand.

I have a dream to put things right,
I will not stand down without a fight.
Clean water for everyone to drink,
I will make the ministers think.

Give the money that people really need,
To solve the problems without the greed.
I have a dream to make things right,
Water for everyone, that's my fight!

Paige Morgan (11)
Cyfarthfa High School, Merthyr Tydfil

I Have A Dream . . .

I have a dream to change the world,
In many different ways,
I have a dream to change the people,
In the living days.

I have a dream to change the schools,
With no bullying,
To keep the rules,
With no arguing.

My dream is as big as the world,
To help children with education
And hope to stop discrimination.

I'll live my life up to everyone's expectations,
But to bring back my devotions,
I'll swim a never-ending ocean,
Only for my dreams to be as big as the world.

Danielle Robins (12)
Cyfarthfa High School, Merthyr Tydfil

I Have A Dream

I have a dream
All people will live in peace,
Bombing and wars will forever cease,
An end to racism of all kinds,
Prejudiced people will change their minds.

I have a dream
There is a cure for cancer,
One day someone will find the answer,
Imagine no poverty or starvation,
It would be a better world for every nation.

Bethan Elinor Pugsley (12)
Cyfarthfa High School, Merthyr Tydfil

I Have A Dream

I have a dream,
A dream where Man can live in peace,
Without the protection of the police.
Where global warming is a thing of the past
And where happiness will always last.
Where people don't have to suffer in pain
And in Africa it will often rain.
A dream where the world will be a better place,
For all mankind, of every race.

Jordan Challis (12)
Cyfarthfa High School, Merthyr Tydfil

I Have A Dream

Maybe one day
There'll be no pain,
No hurt or suffering,
Disease or war.

Maybe there'll be
A golden time,
Almost perfect,
No fighting, but strong love.

Maybe I'll find a place,
Where no one cries,
In desperation,
When they have no hope.

Maybe sometimes,
People will stop to hear,
The little joys of the Earth,
Laughter of happy families.

Maybe . . . just maybe . . .
My dream will come true,
For every night I pray,
For the spark of love,
'n each suffering nation . . .

Hannah Kennedy (12)
Cyfarthfa High School, Merthyr Tydfil

I Have A Dream

I had a dream the other night
Where everyone agreed,
Throughout the world there were no wars,
No poverty, no greed.

The world was such a different place
To the one that we know now,
No guns, no knives, no drugs, no crimes,
No fighting and no rows.

Sadly the world is not like this
If only my dream was true,
There'd be more happiness in the world
And lots of friendship too!

Aimee Jones (13)
Cyfarthfa High School, Merthyr Tydfil

I Have A Dream To Change The World

I have a dream
A dream to change the world
No battles
No wars
No dictators
No followers
No religion and no faiths

A world without confrontation
A world without commiseration
No suicide bombers
Or pointless attacks and deaths

An equal world
With equal people
No hierarchy of life
Where everyone possesses
The same beginning and the same end
One human family.

Carrie-Ann Wheeler (17)
Hartridge High School, Newport

I Have A Dream

Once upon a time,
A speech was made,
By a man who had a dream.

His dream was this,
The world would change
And black and white would be the same.

This man was shot,
In a senseless crime,
He died before his time.

He never saw his dream come true,
But neither have me or you,
Racism still exists.

At the football match,
A sound you'll catch,
A monkey noise from brainless 'fans'.

These fans don't like football,
They like to stir,
They only thing they fan, are the flames of hate.

My dream, you might think has been said before,
But racism still exists,
Even more.

Joseph Phillips (16)
Hartridge High School, Newport

I Have A Dream

My dream world
Is a world without people using cars unless necessary
Fossil fuel flies away by using our cars,
Oil tankers crash and makes endangered species,
I would like to change the world.

Forests falling down, why do we need to?
Less animals, less food, but more endangered species
No! not the food
We don't need the wood but the animals do,
Steel won't run out for years,
I would like to change the world.

Why not recycle? It's not hard,
There are now more endangered species
The Earth is like a giant big bag, don't throw it away,
Glass and packets can last for years,
I would like to change the world.

Factories that we don't need
Pollute the water, we need to act fast,
The animals are going to say goodbye
The water is no longer blue but green,
I would like to change the world.

Think of your pets, the animals
What are our own children going to have for a pet? A spoon?
The world would be a very dim place,
Why do we abuse our pets? They can't understand us,
I would like to change the world.

The ozone layer is being destroyed,
Close your eyes and think about what will happen when it's gone,
The world will dry up and everyone will be gone,
The Earth will be pulled towards the sun
The world is over, *kaboom!*
I would like to change the world.

Leon Cooke (12)
Hartridge High School, Newport

I Have A Dream

Why must we live in a world like this,
Where children starve and live alone?
Yet when we ask for something,
We get it straight away.

When we beg the government for money,
We get it on a golden platter,
Yet when people need it the most,
All they get is what they've got.

They have no idea what it's like to be loved,
Or have a family,
You have loads of friends,
But they have none.

You can open a can of food,
And think nothing of it.
But to someone out there,
It could change a matter of life or death.

Poor, defenceless people
Need our help,
Right here, right now,
Please help them
Before it's too late.

We have a roof over our heads,
Food on the table,
Clothes on our back,
We take these things,
For granted.

Joanne Sana Loder (12)
Hartridge High School, Newport

Have A Dream

I have a dream
To change the world.
To set an example
And make it be seen.

Give to charity
Lend a helping hand.
Help other people
And make the world sound.

Walk down the street tall and proud
Don't take the car.
Pick up the litter
And you're a star.

Do something for the ill
They need to buy pills.
This is what I want
No matter what.

Kara Catherine Campbell (12)
Hartridge High School, Newport

I Have A Dream

I have a dream to
Change the world by
Getting people to recycle everything they can
So the world will be here for longer
So stop and think about your grandchildren
And what you are doing to
Their world.

I have a dream to
Change the world by
Getting people to stop animal cruelty
So animals will be here for longer
So stop. Think about the animal kingdom
And think about what you are doing to
Their world.

I have a dream to
Change the world by
Getting people to stop child cruelty
So humans will be here for longer
So stop. Think about what you are doing to
Their world.

I have a dream to
Change the world by
Getting people to stop racism
So stop. Think. Does it matter if you are white or black?
What's the difference?

So stop. Think about all the things
You have done to the world
Have you made a difference?

Mark O'Connell (12)
Hartridge High School, Newport

I Have A Dream

What's going on in the world today?
Whilst we're getting on with our lives and refusing to pay,
To help the children in Africa and give them food,
How would you feel if that poor child was you?
They are living in poverty and dying from disease,
How can you not help them when they're begging you, please?
I have a dream that it will be better for them someday,
Because I'd rather die than turn my head away.

In the Third World there are too many people crying,
In the Third World there are too many people dying,
Only we can help and we need to pray,
Because at the moment these children can't play,
We need to help to stop their everyday problems,
You have no idea how much that would mean to them,
I have a dream that all this will stop,
I have a dream that they will come out on top.

Yasmin Symonds (15)
Partridge High School, Newport

I Have A Dream . . .

I have a dream to change the world
The people, buildings and environment,
To stop wars erupting and to make life safe . . .
Making the world a more peaceful and happier place.

So many drastic things happening all around the world,
Making *you* and many others afraid,
To walk through the frightening streets, makes your heart beat,
Time just slips away.

Bullying, fighting, rape and murder,
These all take place each day,
Some people are so evil and full of hatred,
Others get by their own way.

Prostitution is such a big thing in life,
Many do it just to keep themselves alive,
Just a little bit of money to make a fresh start,
Not to stay down hurt and cause a crime.

Young children so poor, so skinny and dirty,
Some people just don't care,
The rich and beautiful, so full of glory,
Would you give money to make life fair?

But look on the bright side, having fun with friends and family,
Not all things are that bad,
To have someone to love, to hold and care for,
Just think of all the little things you have.

'What's wrong with some people?' you may ask yourself,
'How can someone be so mean?'
Out of nowhere it hits you, such a cruel attack,
Some people get out still unseen.

Everybody needs a friend when things get tough,
So don't go leaving one behind,
Everybody is different, so stand tall and strong,
Keep that chin of yours up high.

Rachel Stoneman (14)
Hartridge High School, Newport

I Have A Dream

Dehydration, sand and sun
Money, water fights and fun
Two completely different places
Innocent children meeting scary new faces
A world where skin colour and religion matters.

Rich children laughing
Poor children starving
For poor people each day is a fight for survival
Every way we turn through life is delightful
When will poverty end?

A place where food is very rare
I wouldn't like to go there
We waste so much but don't really know
Just how far those people have to go
Some people poor and others rich, everyone is equal.

People frightened, alone and scared
Maybe they wouldn't be if someone cared
Why should people feel this way
Each and every single day?
Life is so unfair.

Sarah Lord (15)
Hartridge High School, Newport

I Have A Dream . . .

I have a dream that society will treat everyone equally
Who are we to judge people?
Everyone has the right to express themselves
Through their appearance
I'd rather be curvy than stick-thin like most celebrities
We all have the right to wear what we like
No one has the right to put us down
No one is really the same colour
We all are individual in our own right
So what if you're overweight?
Nobody is perfect, not even celebrities
People judge other people unfairly
And judge the person before they actually know them
It doesn't matter about your weight, hair colour
What you wear or even your looks
Everyone is beautiful in their own right
I have a dream that society will treat everyone equally!

Kate Fletcher (15)
Hartridge High School, Newport

I Have A Dream

I have a dream that everyone is treated equally in society,
Everyone should have a fair chance
To let their personality shine through,
Their looks, gender or sexuality.
People should have the right to be
Who they want to be and be who they are.
There is so much pressure on people
From the media to look like celebrities
And models, it isn't fair.
If you're not the right skin colour,
Or haven't got the right colour hair,
Not the perfect figure, height or hairstyle,
You're a misfit.
Nobody is perfect,
There will always be one
Person prettier and thinner
Than you, but you're always
Going to be pretty in your own way.
I have a dream that society sees everyone as beautiful.

Kirsty Jones (15)
Hartridge High School, Newport

I Have A Dream!

Bombs dropping,
People shooting,
Why can't it stop?

Children dying,
Mothers crying,
Why can't it stop?

Racism rising,
Terrorists bombing,
Why can't it stop?

Men beating,
Women hiding,
Why can't it stop?

I have a dream,
It will all stop
And the world will live in peace.

Natalie Elphick (15)
Hartridge High School, Newport

I Have A Dream

I have a dream . . .
For everyone to get involved
I have a dream . . .
All questions will be answered.

Why do people go to war . . .
Ending so many short-lived lives?
Why do people break the law . . .
And walk around with pocket knives?

Why is there discrimination . . .
And hatred for different races?
Why is there war between nations . . .
So many fearful faces?

Why do people commit suicide . . .
Because of bullies making themselves feel good?
Why do people do homicide . . .
Not loving everyone like we should?

Dreams are real and can come true . . .
Let's make it happen and not be so blue!

Jodie Harries (15)
Hartridge High School, Newport

I Have A Dream

I have a dream,
War and terrorism will end,
Then everyone can be friends.

I wish everyone would be happy,
Living together in harmony.
It is no life fighting,
Everyone should be warm and inviting.

Why are terrorists bombing places?
If only they could see their victims' faces.
The fear, the pain
Never able to experience life again.

I have a dream,
All different races,
Join hands together
And experience new places.

Laura Richards (15)
Hartridge High School, Newport

I Have A Dream

I have a dream
A dream of equality between all people
What does it matter what colour you are?
Who cares about your posh car?

If only this world was a better place
And everyone had food on their plate
While sitting round a fire in the grate
Let us all get rid of hate.

I have a dream
Of a wonderful time
Complete without crime
While the bells chime.

I have a dream
Where everyone has family and friends
No need to think about trends
Let us take hands
Let us *all* be equal!

Rachel Williams (15)
Hartridge High School, Newport

I Have A Dream

I have a dream,
Why can't we all just be friends?
What's wrong with the world?
We try our best to stop terrorism
But we don't try hard enough
They obviously just don't care
Just 'cause we aren't the same colour
Just 'cause we don't like the same style
Doesn't mean we aren't normal
We still actually care.

Jacqui Gilbert (14)
Hartridge High School, Newport

I Have A Dream . . .

I have as dream
To see the world as a better place
To see a smile on everyone's face
I have a dream.

I have a dream
For no terrorism or racism
For everyone to be equal
I have a dream.

I have a dream
For the grass to be greener
To be light on Earth
I have a dream.

I have a dream
A fantasy
To see all this happen
I have a dream.

But this is not how it seems . . .

Ashleigh Evans (15)
Hartridge High School, Newport

I Have A Dream

I have a dream
One day I'll wake up
Everything will be perfect,
No prejudice or inequality,
Everyone will be judged the same
And be happy,
No one will be scared
To walk alone,
People screaming for joy
Instead of screaming in horror,
Jobs will be equally judged
Male and female,
They will be judged for themselves
Not because they're different,
That is my dream.

Rhiannon Jones (15)
Hartridge High School, Newport

I Have A Dream

I have a dream,
That the world is a perfect place,
Where no one cares what is going on,
They walk on by with a happy face.

I have a dream,
Where everyone is fed,
Every night,
They have a bed.

I have a dream,
Where people have the right to be taught,
Where the world is at peace
And no wars to be fought.

I have a dream,
Our world is great,
But who am I kidding?
It's full of hate!

Lauren Cornwall (14)
Hartridge High School, Newport

I Have A Dream

I have a dream
Where starving, naked children
Find comfort in a warm and loving home
Fresh water flows from every pump
To quench their sun-parched throats
A huge supply of luscious food is available
To stop their everlasting hunger
Where diseases can be helped to cure
And stop ripping families apart
Schools are built, provided with equipment
For children with a thirst for knowledge
Countries which are overflowing with money
Open their greedy eyes and finally do something right
So homeless people can have a place to sleep
And clothes upon their bony backs
I have a dream
Which we can all make reality
If we all just join together
The world can be a better place
Bring a smile to millions of unhappy faces
Let us bring an end to this endless poverty.

Angharad Bishop (15)
Hartridge High School, Newport

I Have A Dream

How can we be civilised
How can we judge
When hundreds of men can
Be killed over a racist grudge?

Where is the love for which we pray?
Why do we just waste the day
Sitting and joking and having a laugh
Whilst some homeless child can't have a bath?

Why do we sit and have a joke
When a poor African woman is starting to choke?
Choking on tears of pain and fear
As her child's life is all but near.

I have a dream
That one day the world that we live in
Will be 'normal' again.

Shaunna Fallon (15)
Hartridge High School, Newport

I Have A Dream!

Everybody has a dream of being OK,
Violence, rape, prostitutes, no way.
Being ill and afraid is not a dream,
To be rich, powerful and strong is not a scene.
A dream is to be healthy, alive and safe,
There ain't no better dream that believing in faith.

Religions, colour and life are all the same,
Why make it difficult for people who aren't to blame?
Wars are horrific, commanding and scary,
Who wants to be alone thinking, *oh Mary?*
Everyone is equal and together as one,
Having a laugh and reasoning with fun.

Cruelty and slave labour shouldn't be done,
Everyone should be together, eating a cream bun.
Dreams are real and dreams can come true,
Come make it happen and don't be so blue.
Be loving and caring, don't be so cunning,
Families and friends are just so loving.

Sarah Spruce (14)
Hartridge High School, Newport

I Have A Dream

I have a dream that I could walk down the street
And not be ignored by the people I meet.
Tell me, why is it that everyone frowns?
And walks on by with their heads hanging down?
Is life all that bad? Just think for a while
's it really a chore to break into a smile?
There's illness cured and lives saved every day
And fires put out and criminals locked away.
Yet we only hear of the bad and never the good
I think that good deeds are misunderstood.
I know that there are crimes and doings of wrong
And although I wish all bad things were gone
We need to hear less about the troubles and strife
And we all need to look on the bright side of life!

Grace Phillips (13)
Hartridge High School, Newport

I Have A Dream

My dream
A dream to transfigure the world
To view it warm and welcoming
To whiff the scent of happiness spring forth
To heed the rings of bells that echo freedom
To feel the acceptance rush through my veins
To relish the sacred sweetness of the people
My dream
Is for everlasting tranquillity
Between races, sexuality, gender, style and age
To demolish the pain and angst
To embrace the reality that we are unique
And to realise it's fitting
For the world to be uncut
For them, the people's tears to stop
For everyone on Earth to be delighted
That is what I dream.

Rosie Hyden (13)
Hartridge High School, Newport

I Had A Dream

I had a dream
That could change the world

Go back in time
So that there were no horrible wars
Racism did not exist
Children were not living on the smelly streets.

There was no global warming
No one living in poverty
No streets full of rubbish
No more horrid crime and dreadful murders.

And everything was OK with the world
But . . .

Wars have gone on
Racism does exist
Children do live on the dreaded streets
We have global warming
And more and more people are living in poverty.

It's time to change.

Zoe Whant (13)
Hartridge High School, Newport

I Have A Dream

I have a dream that one day everything will be OK
And that all the hassle and worries will all be washed away,
I would love to just walk down the street
And be happy with what I see,
But we all know what the world is coming to be,
Litter everywhere and people dying as we speak,
People getting raped and murdered every single week,
The world is not fair, we are living in Hell
And we are polluting this Earth, you can tell by the smell,
The way we are living is surely wrong,
If we carry on like this, the world won't last long,
There are rumours that soon enough the world is going to end
And it is going to happen, we shouldn't pretend,
If we do not stop pollution right now,
We will all be thinking why and how,
Why is it like this and how can it be,
That the water levels are rising in the sea?
As I stand here watching the world go round,
Why does it always get me down?
Is it supposed to be like this?

Abby Evans (13)
Hartridge High School, Newport

I Have A Dream . . .

Black and Asian will be OK
And their lives will never get taken away,
Riots and wars in Birmingham,
People say it's over, but knowing it has just begun,
People as young as eleven walking with knives,
Taking away each other's lives,
I see the world coming to an end,
But what we need is to all become friends,
Tears and sorrow
Anger and pain
But all we need to do
Is to start all over again,
Being afraid to walk down the street
Not knowing who we are going to meet,
Mothers and fathers feel the pain
Knowing their kids are never coming back again.

Ciccona Taylor (14)
Hartridge High School, Newport

I Have A Dream . . .

That everyone will be OK
And nothing will ever take them away,
Heartache and tears will no longer be around,
Tears and pain will one day make us proud.

The place is starting to smell, as you can tell,
Everywhere you look, all around is litter,
Nature is dying away,
People are starting to help, but always tend to stray.

There are illnesses cured every day,
Murderers and rapists all locked away,
Family and friends are all together,
Thinking about one another.

There's war and terror all over the world,
I have a dream for peace and harmony,
Everyone needs to be strong
To help the world get along.

Lauren Clarke (14)
Hartridge High School, Newport

I Have A Dream

I have a dream that the unique universe will become
  a profound place

H appy faces everywhere
A ll racism to be demolished
V iolence will become extinct
E veryone equally sharing rights

A dream hoping to come true

D estroying the world, is what we are doing
R emembering the disgusting smell of burning fuels
  and rethinking about the new fresh air
E ducation can help your future
A ll pollution to be destroyed
M aking your dream come true

I have a dream
That all my dreams will come true
For a better world.

Jodie Chapman (14)
Hartridge High School, Newport

I Have A Dream

Abandoned,
That's how they feel,
Left alone without a hope.

Neglected,
That's what they are,
Just lonely children left to starve.

Deprived,
In need of help,
Poor, needy children who need a better life.

Heartbroken,
Miserable and disappointed,
No love to get them through their day.

Hopeful,
Reassure their hopes
And rebuild their long-lost dreams.

Vulnerable,
In danger of dying,
Loss of life due to abandonment.

Children being dumped on the streets,
They are lonely and left to fight for themselves,
Give them hope and raise some money,
Let's make the world a better place.

Bethan Jones (13)
Hartridge High School, Newport

I Have A Dream

I have a dream that we can get those
Exquisite birds back into our forests
That we can stop all of the global warming
And recycle all of the rubbish we leave
On the streets so that we do not destroy our Earth.

I have a dream that poverty never existed
And we have a cure for all major diseases
So everyone can live to their full extent.

I have a dream that race will not come into account
Everyone is treated fairly
But at this moment in time
None of this is happening!

That is my dream.

Mitchell Reid (13)
Hartridge High School, Newport

Words To Change The World

I have a dream to change the world
To change the world from what we see
From what we touch, taste and hear
I have a dream to change the world.

I have a dream to rid the world
Of people who are rapists and who bully
To rid the world of these vicious people
For innocent people take their lives
To end their torture and cruelty.

I have a dream to demolish all diseases
Cancer, AIDS and HIV too,
For all the drugs and antidotes
Only some things ever work
But if you're lucky, you can thank the men in white coats.

I have a dream to make the world a better place
For people rich, poor, young or old
To change the world, to save the world
Just for you and me
If you want to save your home, recycling is the key.

I have a dream to help countries in need
Africa, Asia and India
Those countries that are suffering
In poverty, wars and world hunger
But most of all, ecological destruction.

But at this moment, this is just a dream.

Zenith Jones (13)
Hartridge High School, Newport

Have A Dream

Everybody should feel wanted,
Everybody should care,
Everybody should recycle,
For our world to share.

Child abuse is really wrong,
Think how the child must feel,
Upset, annoyed, sad and sorrowful,
That just cannot be real.

I wish there was no harming,
No vandalism or breaking,
Even people think they are hard,
By racism.

This is our world,
Please don't throw it away,
You can recycle almost anything,
It could change our day.

I have a dream,
It's about babies,
Why do people feel so angry at them?
Why can't they just be happy?

No it has come to the end,
All about my dreams,
I really hope they come true
To be really nice and not mean.

Leanne Bale (11)
Hartridge High School, Newport

I Have A Dream

I had a dream of the world
A peaceful world and free of pollution
Everyone was wanted
No one was alone!

Vandalism, racism, that was all gone!
Loving and recycling that was here instead
Cruelty and crimes, they had disappeared
Life was a better place!

Child abuse had stopped
Loving had started
Children had fabulous parents
Mums and dads and nans and bampys.

Child abuse, please stop
I really, really hope
I feel inside my heart
How the child can cope!

No more bullying
Why do they do it?
They must think they're hard
To hurt people in such terrible ways.

People think
Cruelty and crimes are cute!
They're *not!*
They are just crazy!

Natalie Michelle West (12)
Hartridge High School, Newport

I Have A Dream

I yearn that there is no RSPCA
So that the animals are not abused
I envisage that every child does not have to hide
And isn't assaulted in a place that they think is safe.

I wish that racism was a thing of the past
And countries will form together as one
I dream that there is no such thing as money
So you and I don't have to pay for life's luxuries.

Why is it so unrelenting
To help those in need?
Next time think about you
In your time of need?

At night I look in the sky
And wonder if others are too
But sometimes I wonder
If you care as much as I do.

Shannon Breslin (12)
Hartridge High School, Newport

I Have A Dream

I have a dream
A dream to change this world,
Racism never, ever existed,
Bullying was never heard of,
Oh, that world would be great!

I have a dream
A very *big* dream
That medication was free
No matter your age or illness
You would get treatment every day
In every single way.

I have a dream
Stupid it may seem
People recycled their cans
So we would have all different plans.

I have a dream
To turn this world around
So that guns, robbers and murderers
Were far below the ground.

I have a dream
That every child has someone to hold
Instead of being stranded outside
In the freezing cold.

Bonnie Arlett (12)
Hartridge High School, Newport

I Have A Dream

I have a dream to make the world a safer, better
And more helpful place
I need people to take care of dogs
Because they're not just for Christmas but for life
The same goes for all pets and all kinds of animals.

I have a dream to have no bullies
To give everyone a happy life
Don't forget, if you laugh with a bully
That means *you* are a bully
I would stop all racism so people will not get upset.

I have a dream to make everyone have a satisfied soul
I would let everyone go to Heaven
And not to horrible Hell.

I have a dream to have no litter in the city
Or anywhere in the world
And it would be a clean world
With no adorable animals dying
Just think what a world of helpful humans
And lovely animals could be like
The world would be like living in a tidier
Better and more comfortable place.

Joel Gibbons (12)
Hartridge High School, Newport

I Have A Dream

I have a dream
A dream where people will not murder each other
And where parents will not abuse their children
Think about all the people who have lost someone close to them
Imagine if someone close to you was brutally murdered.

I have a dream
A dream where there is no hunger
Where everyone will have fantastic food to eat
And water to drink.

I have a dream
A dream where there are enough cures for every illness
Where everyone will be healthy
And no one will die of dreadful diseases
Imagine your mother with breast cancer.

I have a dream
A dream where everyone has a home
A dream where no one is left out on the street.

I have a dream
A dream where there are no wars
Where there is no bombing
Where everyone gets along.

Oliver Griffiths (12)
Hartridge High School, Newport

I Have A Dream

The world is a spectacular place
Many beautiful things to see
So why are we destroying it?

In many years time
There could be an end
An end to this great planet.

Acid rain falls like sharp needles
Pollution poisoning the air
People littering the land
Our environment is being destroyed.

I have a dream that we can change this
That the air will be fresh and clean
Litter to be recycled
Splash! The rain falls acid-free
No dramatic changes in the weather.

We can all help to change our world
For the better
I have a dream that we can save
Our spectacular, sensational planet!

Hannah Milne (13)
Cartridge High School, Newport

I Have A Dream . . .

I have a dream to be rich
So I can help people in life.

I have a dream to be married to someone cute
To spend my life with him forever.

I have a dream that no one
Will pick on me in life.

I have a dream that people
Will be kind to animals and not evil to them.

I have a dream that my gran will be here
To watch me growing up in life.

I have a dream that there will be
No sexism in life.

I have a dream that no one will have cancer
And if they can be treated with full support.

Lucy Webb (13)
Hartridge High School, Newport

I Have A Dream

I have a dream that people are smiling
Because they are happy in this world
I have a dream we can play football all the time
I have a dream to meet all my friends again
I have a dream there is no violence in the world
I have a dream that it is always warm
I have a dream that there are no bad words in this world
I have a dream to help my mum when I am older
I have a dream there's no swearing in the world.

Issa Silemani (13)
Hartridge High School, Newport

I Have A Dream . . .

I have a dream . . .
There is no bullying
People can walk around school safely
I have a dream . . .
That I could meet my brother
One more time before he died
I have a dream . . .
To stop animal cruelty
I have a dream . . .
To win the Lotto
To help my family
And to help the world
I have a dream . . .
There is no war
People will not fear guns
And not see innocent people being killed
I have a dream . . .
That I can see the world in space
To see the white, silky clouds
And the beautiful blue water
I have a dream . . .
That I can stop racism
So that people can be seen
The way I see the world
I have a dream . . .
To live in Germany again
The summers are beautiful and hot
And the winters are pure white
Not a colour in sight

Riah Goodison (14)
Hartridge High School, Newport

I Have A Dream

I have a dream
That no matter what colour or race
We will all be treated the same
Every child has the right to learn
And go to school
Every family has enough food and water
Not now and then, but every day
Not to be afraid of your next-door neighbour
To be able to live in peace
To respect each other's differences
In every single way
I have a dream
Someday it will come true.

Ellis Anderson (12)
Hartridge High School, Newport

I Have A Dream

I have a dream
That we live in peace
I have a dream
There is no war
I have a dream
That everyone is kind to one another
I have a dream
There is no cruelty
I have a dream
That no one judges anyone
I have a dream
There is no racism
I have a dream
There is no cruelty to animals.

Shannon Jones (14)
Hartridge High School, Newport

I Have A Dream

I have a dream
That racism stops
So we can't judge each other
By our colour or how we look

In my world
I wish there wasn't any abuse
To children, women and men
And that we could get treated the same
And all get along

There would be no wars in my world
Because everyone would get along with each other

There would be no rape in my world
Because people get hurt and it's wrong

There would be no jealousy in my world
Because people would all have the same money and clothes

In my world
I wish there wasn't any poverty
And we all had the same things.

There would be no bullying in my world
Because our education matters

There would be no robbery in my world
Because people would lose special and expensive things

There would be no disease in my world
Because now there are some which we can't cure
Because they are too bad

There would be no animal cruelty in my world
Because all the animals would be loved and cared for.

Rebecca Bill (12)
Hartridge High School, Newport

I Have A Dream!

People are all the same
Don't treat it like a game
People are big
People are small
Some are black
And some are white
People should all be treated the same
Let's not be lame
Some people are fat
Some people are thin
Let's all rejoice
Ourselves within
People are all the same
Don't treat it like a game.

Nikki Fleming
Hartridge High School, Newport

I Have A Dream

I have a dream
That one day racism will be gone
Black and white people
Will one day come together
And rise to the top of the world.

I have a dream
That one day war will disappear into the distance
Different cultures should put differences aside
And become friends
Put down the weapons and let all the fighting stop
Let's all come together and make our world better.

Steven Farley (14)
Hartridge High School, Newport

I Have A Dream

I have a dream that there
Will be no more war
Throw all the guns away
Let us enjoy each day

Let the fighting stop
Turn on the clock
Throw the bombs away
A new way for a new day

Why are soldiers fighting?
Let's get along
Let's start again
Let everyone be equal
Then maybe this world
Wouldn't be such a mess.

Jenna Allman (14)
Hartridge High School, Newport

I Have A Dream

I have a dream that everyone
Will be equal
No matter who they are
And where they are from.

Black, white, rich or poor
People should be treated equally
Stop the hate, there's no need
Why are we making black people plead?

I have a dream that everyone
Will be equal
No matter who they are.

Chelsea Macdonald (13)
Hartridge High School, Newport

I Have A Dream

I have a dream
Black and white people can be friends
Stop hating each other
That the world will be free from racist people
Everyone is the same
It doesn't matter what you look like or where you're from
Take a leaf out of the opposite colour's book
See what it feels like to be judged.

I have a dream
That poverty will stop
No more children lying in the streets
Being left for dead
We should help as many people as we can
By giving money
Save people's lives.

I have a dream
Of a violence-free world
Help each other and take care of each other
Be helpful to others and they will help you.

I have a dream!

Kimberley Berry (13)
Hartridge High School, Newport

I Have A Dream

I have a dream
That people should stop racism
I think that all people
Should be treated the same way.

I have a dream
To stop people from littering
Throwing rubbish on the floor
It's bad and they shouldn't do it.

I have a dream
For the world to be a better place
For everybody to be friends
To not fall out and have wars.

Hollie Short (12)
Hartridge High School, Newport

I Have A Dream

I have a dream
To stop the wars, so people can't die
So their families can't fear and cry.

There's no need for weapons
What a horrible creation
So I hope you think about this small conversation.

So throw away the war planes
So the other people cannot be in pain
There's no need for violence
So stop and think in a minute of silence.

There's no need for war
So sit down and relax
Go to Greece
And make world peace!

Michael McLoughlin (11)
Hartridge High School, Newport

I Have A Dream

I have a dream
That people will stop doing graffiti on walls
I have a dream
That there will be no wars
I have a dream
That there will be no bullying or global warming
I have a dream
That the world will be clean and tidy
I have a dream
That the shops will stop selling cigarettes
I have a dream
That people on the streets will have a house
I have a dream
That people will stop selling drugs.

Aaron Podmore (11)
Hartridge High School, Newport

I Have A Dream

I have a dream
That young or old people
Shouldn't take drugs
It's a waste of life
It's not lucky.

I have a dream
That they should stop *now!*
They're ruining it for the country
Even town.

I have a dream
That we stop, think and try to be happy
By meeting someone and not taking drugs
They are wasting your money
Use your common sense!

Stevie Ridler (12)
Hartridge High School, Newport

Why Drugs?

I have a dream
That people will stop smoking
And stop taking drugs

If there was no one selling drugs
The world would be a better place.

Families would stay together
Friendship wouldn't break apart
No drugs, no drink, no smoking
This is my dream.

Jordan Ellul (11)
Hartridge High School, Newport

Drugs

Drugs, drugs everywhere
People who take them just don't care

People take it, don't you know
Cannabis and even blow

Don't you know this stuff is illegal
They say you fly like a seagull

Stop it, that's what I say
Otherwise you will pay.

Brett Rosser (13)
Hartridge High School, Newport

I Have A Dream

I have a dream
Of a world without war
Where everyone lives in peace
Not a world where people are dying
For no reason at all.

I have a dream
Of a world without drugs
Where people aren't destroying their lives
Or old smelly mugs.

. have a dream
Of a world without hunger
Where everyone has meat to eat
Especially the younger.

I have a dream
Of a world with better health care
With no sickness and no disease
With cured people here and there.

I have a dream
Of a world without global warming
Where the Earth isn't being polluted
No need for a nuclear warning.

I have a dream
Where people care for others
Where none of us are left home alone
Where no one's fighting with their brothers.

I have a dream
Of a world without violence
Where no one is fighting in the streets
With everyone living in peace and silence.

Vaughan Hughes (14)
Hartridge High School, Newport

I Have A Dream

I have a dream that everyone will be respected equally
Adults, children and teenagers
I have a dream that people will not judge you
By the answer you give, like not judging a book by its cover
I have a dream that people will not call you things
Just for what you enjoy
I have a dream that we will all be respected
For our views and opinions
I have a dream that you should not be judged
By your past, but by your present time in life
I have a dream that racism doesn't exist
Because colours cause chaos
I have a dream that we do not take things for granted
I have a dream that we can live in peace
I have a dream that there is *no* bullying
I have a dream that people don't label people by their clothes
Or music, but by their personality
I have a dream today.

Harriet Smith (13)
Hartridge High School, Newport

I Have A Dream

I have a dream that racism is a thing of the past
And we all have respect for each other
I have a dream that you have respect for who you are now
Not what you have done in the past
I have a dream that diseases are cured
And other life threats are gone
I have a dream that everyone is treated fairly
And not bullied
I have a dream that there are no poor people
Or rich people in the world
I have a dream that there are no labels in the world
I have a dream that there is no crime,
Murder or evil people in the world
I have a dream that child abuse stops forever
I have a dream that animal abuse stops fast!

Ellesse Buss (13)
Hartridge High School, Newport

I Have A Dream

I have a dream that people don't label us for what we like
                                              and what we do
I have a dream that everyone is treated equally
I have a dream that none of us gets judged by our past
I have a dream that there is no racism in this world
I have a dream that there is no poverty in the world
I have a dream that all the bullies get punished for what they do
I have a dream that there's no pollution
I have a dream that we don't get judged by what we think
I have a dream that people don't look at us
For what our colour on our skin is.

Carla Galamas (12)
Hartridge High School, Newport

I Have A Dream

I have a dream that everyone treats each other the same
I have a dream that there is no graffiti
I have a dream that there will be no bullying
I have a dream we don't get judged by who we are
I have a dream we don't get judged at first sight
I have a dream that we don't get judged by labels
I have a dream that everyone respects each other
I have a dream that people can listen to what music they want
I have a dream that people don't wreck the environment
I have a dream that there is no terrorism.

Lewis Clarke (13)
Hartridge High School, Newport

I Have A Dream

I have a dream that war and conquest will stop

H ave a good life not a terrible one
A nyone in this world hates terror
V ery hard life to live when bullying is happening
E veryone knows bullying is wrong

A ny person should know that it's true

D ying people every day that is nothing unusual
R ight, let's stop it, *full stop*
E very person should conquer their fears
A nyone who is old should get some respect
M ay I wish people a good life.

Sam Davies (13)
Hartridge High School, Newport

I Have A Dream

There would be no racism because white and black are together
There would be no bullying to anyone
And we would be kind and loving to each other
There would be no sexism because of who we are
There would be no abuse to children by their parents
There would be no murders so then people could walk
Down the street without fear
There would be no poverty and people would have food
And a roof over their heads
There would be no robbery and people could keep their doors open
Without anyone getting robbed
There would be no cruelty to animals
There would be no famine or death
There would be no war and people
Wouldn't have to worry about dying
There would be no smoking because it's a bad example to children.

Hannah Shingler (11)
Hartridge High School, Newport

I Have A Dream . . .

I have a dream everybody gets along with each other
I have a dream that everybody is treated equally
I have a dream everybody in class is quiet
I have a dream there are only two lessons a day
I have a dream nobody will get hurt
I have a dream war will end
I have a dream the school will fall down
I have a dream that racism will stop
I have a dream there will be no robbery
I have a dream that I will not die.

Matthew Tucker (11)
Hartridge High School, Newport

I Have A Dream

I have a dream that
Everyone can be treated equally
That there is no border dividing us all
That everything is as peaceful as a stream.

' have a dream that
Race doesn't matter
And we can all just get along
Everyone should respect each other
That we could all mix like strawberries and cream.

I have a dream that
We can all just become friends
It doesn't matter what clothes you wear
What you look like or your hair
Just remember who you are
Keep you head up and you'll go far.

Laura Day (15)
Hartridge High School, Newport

Words To Change The World

I have a dream to change the world
From what it has come to be
In my mind I imagine it to be better
Than what I really see.

All the pollution in the air
It really seems like no one cares
We all should come together in harmony
And change the world from what it has come to be.

Bullying and racism are in the air
It makes life seem like it isn't fair
For all the bickering and arguments that come around
I am glad our friends are here supporting us all year round.

I have a dream to change the world
To annihilate homophobia
I want to make the world a better place
So no person lives in fear.

This is all a dream for me
That I wish to make true one day.

Lauren Symonds (14)
Hartridge High School, Newport

I Have A Dream

I have a dream of peace and tranquillity
Of a world without fear or tyranny
Where all people walk hand in hand
Through forest, over mountains and on sand.

A world without famine or disease
Where hot summers have a gentle breeze
Whilst bears are peacefully sleeping
The willows are no longer weeping.

But the world is an evil place
Where you're picked on because of your face
If there was just something I could do
If *only* my dream would come true.

Simon Fisher (14)
Hartridge High School, Newport

I Have A Dream

I have a dream
That the world is calm, a peaceful kind of place,
Where the birds are singing
And the trees are swaying
And a smile is on everyone's face.

I have a dream
All disease is cured,
No matter what the cost,
Because we're all human and have our rights,
Without them we would be lost.

I have a dream
There were no wars,
No riots or attacks,
When they say stop, both sides quit,
No one goes behind any backs.

I have a dream
It's not at all about colour,
You can be any religion,
Nobody ever judges people
For the beliefs they believe in.

I have a dream
That all children would have homes,
Not sad and lonely crying,
These little faces would light up,
If they had a bed to lie in.

This is my dream
Hopefully it will come true one day
It would make the world a better place,
In every single little way.

Shanté Seivwright (13)
Hartridge High School, Newport

Words To Change The World

I have a dream that one day the world can be free
Free from racism and pollution
With no borders to be hassled with
Or no cares about the future
If we recycle the world will smell much better
And our countryside or coastal views
Will not be ruined by rubbish that's stacked to the sky
There are few things we can change instantly
And there are few words that make us change our minds
But if we all recycle, the future will be better for us all
The fallen trees in the forests or woods
That once stood proud and tall
The homeless animals who have been driven away
By the man with the chainsaw who chops and chops all day
Tall trees now fall like dominoes
The evergreens of the world now vanish
That was my dream and I hope it comes true.

Rhys Peters (14)
Hartridge High School, Newport

I Have A Dream . . .

I have a dream
That one day you can turn over a new page
And breast cancer will be treated seriously
No matter your circumstances
It should not be like a lucky dip
To get this illness cured
Give the drug to everyone.

I have a dream
That one day I will wake up
And cars and steelworks will be eradicated
And I hope to wake up one day
To find pollution has ended.

When you look upon life
Life should be good
Do you realise what we
Are doing to this world?

Natasha Marasco (14)
Hartridge High School, Newport

I Have A Dream

I have a dream
That child abuse
Must stop!
Think about family and friends
Would you like it?

I have a dream
That everyone will
Have a warm place to live
Heated food on a plate, *gulp!*

I have a dream
That everyone will be
A big family
No war!
World peace!

I have a dream
That everyone recycles
We are running
Out of land to
Put our rubbish
Imagine your grandchildren!

I have a dream
That horrible hunting shall *stop now!*
Animal cruelty shall finish
Think about your own animals.

I wish, I wish
I hope you wish too
Would you like it
If that was you?

Paige Attewell (12)
Hartridge High School, Newport

Equality

I am your friend
So you tell me this . . .
Why are we treating these people so diff?
Just because of their skin colour
This is so lame
Skin colour doesn't matter
We are all the same
It's not what we see
For none of this is what I dream.

People look different
That's what makes us stand out
Stop the bullying people
It makes you a lout.

So cut it out
There's more to life
Let's have equality
Let's get it right.

It's inside that counts
No what we see
I want equality
I have this dream.

Georgina Powell (14)
Hartridge High School, Newport

I Have A Dream

I have a dream to stop bullying, it drives people crazy
If you had a friend and he was getting bullied every day
Would you stand and stare
Or would you stop and care?

If there were less bullies in the world
There would be less sadness
So please, stop bullying
Stop bullying!

It's not cool
It's just being a fool
So tackle bullying
Before it tackles you.

Lewys Manley (11)
Hartridge High School, Newport

I Have A Dream

Don't take drugs, it's not very good
It can harm you, so stop when you should
Drugs are so bad, they can harm your heart
Stop them now or they'll tear you apart.

Can you stop this thing because it doesn't get you anywhere
Stop calling names and take in the care
It doesn't matter what shape, how you look or your hair
It doesn't matter what you look like, so don't stare.

Ben Churcher (12)
Hartridge High School, Newport

I Have A Dream

I have a dream to stop bullying,
To make the school a better place,
If you get bullied, the best thing to do,
Is tell a teacher,
Or they will carry on bullying you,
Stop bullying or you will have no friends.

How do you think the person feels
When you are bullying?
You wouldn't like it,
If you were getting bullied!
You would be upset, they are upset,
So leave them alone.

Bullying is wrong,
You only bully other people because,
You are bored.
Don't bully each other,
It is nasty,
Don't be a bully, be a friend!

Claire-Louise Trigg (12)
Hartridge High School, Newport

I Have A Dream

A dream to stop poverty,
To feed the starving people of the world,
To give them warmth and food.

I have a dream to stop the war,
To make everyone friends,
To stop the fights and rows,
I wish it was no more.

I have a dream to stop racism,
To make black and white people friends
And not enemies,
What difference does it make
What colour we are?

I have a dream for the world
To be a better place
For everyone to be treated the same.

Amy Peterson (12)
Hartridge High School, Newport

I Have A Dream

To one day see my mum again
To have world peace
That everyone was treated the same
No fighting
No murders
No wars
That my mum and dad get back together
When I die I want to go to Heaven
I have a dream that I get a good education
I have a dream that I get my anger sorted out.

James Blandford (12)
Hartridge High School, Newport

I Have A Dream

There would be no bullying because there's no need to bully
There would be no sexism because it doesn't matter
Whether you're a boy or girl
There shouldn't be abuse because there's no need to be abusive
People should walk round the streets and not be scared
There shouldn't be rape because it's wrong
There shouldn't be drugs because they can kill you
There shouldn't be war because every country should be friends
There shouldn't be smoking because you could get cancer and die
There shouldn't be robbery because people can rob expensive things
There shouldn't be murder because you die and it's wrong.

Paul Stoneman (12)
Hartridge High School, Newport

I Have A Dream

I have a dream that there is no racism so no one will get beaten
For what they are or what the colour of their skin is
I have a dream no one gets bullied
I have a dream there is no jealousy
The world would be a much better place without jealousy
I have a dream that all wars stop
I have a dream there is no such thing as smoking so no one dies
I have a dream that no one is scared of rape
I have a dream that no one is ashamed of sexism
I have a dream no one robs anyone for money
I have a dream no one gets diseases.

Kieron Campbell (11)
Hartridge High School, Newport

I Have A Dream

I have a dream
That poverty isn't tolerated
And people have all the same amount of money.

I have a dream
That murder isn't an issue
And people have something else to do.

I have a dream
That terrorism doesn't exist
And people aren't jealous of other countries.

Gregory Baker (12)
Hartridge High School, Newport

My Dream Is . . .

For people not to worry
I want people to be nice to one another
And to help one another.

For people not to fear walking down the street
And not to worry about rape or murder.

For children not to worry about abuse
From their parents.

For animals not to worry
About dying or hunger.

For people not to use drugs or attack other people
In any way to do with drugs.

For people not to worry about war
War should not be a threat!

For people not to smoke
Because people can die.

No racism because we should
All be the same.

To live peacefully.

For people not to commit suicide
And for people to like who they are.

Megan Bliss (12)
Hartridge High School, Newport

I Have A Dream

I have a dream that there is no racism
White and black should be allowed together.
War should stop. Britain should get along
With other countries.
In my world, my dream would be no earthquakes
Because people die and homes are destroyed.
There should be no smoking
Because people die of cancer.
I have a dream to not be cruel to animals
And kill them for food.
There would be no rape, it's wrong and bad.
There would be no robbery
Because people take expensive things like cars
I have a dream there's no murder because it's wrong
There would be no diseases - too many people die of diseases
Because we can't cure them
Sexism would be wrong
Men and women should get along.
I have a dream.

Liam Codd (12)
Hartridge High School, Newport

I Have A Dream

I have a dream
That there will be no racism
And black and white people will get along.

> I have a dream
> That there will be no abuse
> Because people get hurt.

I have a dream
That there will be no murders
Because children lose their mums and dads.

> I have a dream
> That there will be no pollution
> Because there are bins everywhere.

I have a dream
That people won't rob
Because people won't have expensive things.

> I have a dream
> That people will be able to walk
> In the street and not be afraid.

I have a dream
That people don't smoke
So they don't have lung cancer.

> I have a dream
> That people will be nice to their animals
> And care for them.

I wish that there were no disasters
Then the world would be perfect.

I hope all my dreams come true!

Bethan Spruce (11)
Hartridge High School, Newport

I Have A Dream

I have a dream that the world is free of poverty
I have a dream that the world is free from racism
And terrorism has stopped
I have a dream that war has ended
People stop being prejudiced
Let's stop drugs and fights
Let us have political rights
I have a dream that everyone is treated the same way.

Jake David Thomas (13)
Hartridge High School, Newport

I Have A Dream

I have a dream that there are no drugs in the world
I have a dream that we are all treated equally
I have a dream that bullying is stopped
I have a dream there's no terrorism
I have a dream that there are no diseases in the world
I have a dream there are no weapons in the world
I have a dream that we're not labelled
I have a dream that there is no racism
I have a dream for no more wars
I have a dream for an end to war and hunger
I have a dream for world peace.

Joshua Poole (13)
Hartridge High School, Newport

I Have A Dream!

I have a dream
That everybody is treated the same
I have a dream
That nobody is labelled
I have a dream
That there is no racism at all
I have a dream
That nobody gets judged
I have a dream
That people do what they want
I have a dream
That nobody gets bullied
I have a dream
That people have access to anything
I have a dream
That there is no poverty
I have a dream
That nobody pollutes the air
I have a dream!

Louise Evans (13)
Hartridge High School, Newport

I Have A Dream

I have a dream
That one day everyone will be equal - no racism
I have a dream
That racist words will not be a part of our language
I have a dream
That one day labels like 'chav', 'sweaty', 'Goth' or 'Emo' did not exist
We're all equal!
I have a dream
That one day we will not be picked on
If we are a different race or religion
I have a dream
That one day sexist language does not exist.

We're all equal!

Jason Little (12)
Hartridge High School, Newport

I Have A Dream!

I have a dream that people will not be judged
By the colour of their skin or the clothes they wear.
I have a dream that no one should be treated differently
To anyone else.
I have a dream that there is no racism in the world.
I have a dream that children, women and men
Do not act on what they see on the television.
I have a dream that there are no diseases
That can kill people or be passed on to others.
I have a dream that people should not take their lives
Because of others.
I have a dream that there is no terrorism in the world.
I have a dream that people should treat each other with *respect!*
I have a dream that there is no violence in the world!

Charlotte Lewis (13)
Hartridge High School, Newport

I Have A Dream

I have a dream that there is no cruelty to animals
Because they are living creatures like us.
I have a dream that there is no rape
Because no man or woman should be scared of rape.
I have a dream that there is no war
We should live in peace and harmony.
I have a dream that no poverty is great because if everyone
Had the same amount of money, people would not get robbed.
I have a dream that robbery is no more
Because you shouldn't be jealous of anyone.
! have a dream smoking is banned
Because people get lung cancer and are dying.
I have a dream that sexism is not allowed
Because women can do all men can do.
I have a dream pollution is gone
Because if it stays, people in the future might get cancer.
I have a dream that there is no bullying
Because people get scared and some commit suicide.
I have a dream that there is no racism
Because everyone's the same, it's just different skin colour
Which doesn't matter!

Scott Milne (11)
Hartridge High School, Newport

I Have A Dream

I have a dream
That there is no drug abuse.
I have a dream
That there is no murder.
I have a dream
That there is no rape so no man, woman or child
Will fear walking in the street.
I have a dream
That there is no sexism.
I have a dream
That there is no smoking or drinking of alcohol.
I have a dream
That there is no bullying.
I have a dream
That there is no jealousy.
I have a dream
That teachers believe everyone.
I have a dream
That money grows on trees.
I have a dream
That no one has enemies and everyone is friends!

Ammi Ricci (12)
Hartridge High School, Newport

I Have A Dream

I have a dream
That nobody gets hurt when they're walking home at night.
I have a dream
That at night, when people get drunk they don't cause violence.
I have a dream
Homeless people have homes to live in.
I have a dream
That all war does not exist.
I have a dream
That everyone is happy and not worried about getting judged.
I have a dream
That no one gets judged on the way they look.
I have a dream
That people aren't killed over their skin colour.
I have a dream
That drug abuse never happens in the first place.
I have a dream
That mugging old people stops.

Steven Taylor (12)
Hartridge High School, Newport

Critty Crime

You should not break the law
The law is there to stop you
From doing the wrong things
You should always stick to the rules
The law is like
A guideline to help you
The law is there for a reason
And it goes for everyone
Not for individuals
The law is like the rules in school
So stick to them
There are laws all over the world
So it is not just us.

Ryan Everett (12)
Hartridge High School, Newport

The World

T he world is an evil place
H urricanes destroying the world
E vil terrorists bombing cities

W ars all over the world
O ur children are affected
R ivers are being polluted by people
L onely people are getting bullied
D evastation of poverty . . .

Gareth Chorley-Davies (13)
Hartridge High School, Newport

Society

Society is you
No one else but you
It doesn't matter what other people think
Or what you think
On the inside you're beautiful.

No need to listen to bullies or magazines
And there's no need to have surgery
So let your hair down
And accept that you're beautiful.

Jessica Morgan (13)
Hartridge High School, Newport

The World

What is going on in this world?
Saddam Hussein has put some tears in the world
But there are no plasters to cover it!

There is too much pollution in the world
If we don't recycle
There won't be any world left!

The world would be a better place without bullies
They just do it to show off
And think they are better than the rest!

I have a dream!
That there will be no tears in the world
That there will be no bullies
And the world will be a better society!

Dominique Hackwood (13)
Hartridge High School, Newport

I Have A Dream

I have a dream
Men and women are treated equally
I have a dream
Black and white people stand tall together
I have a dream
That men, women and children never live in fear
I have a dream
That there are no differences between animals and people
We are all happy
I have a dream
Everyone has money, a good job and welcome to learn
I have a dream
People will not suffer for the decision that their Prime Minister has
made
I have a dream
People do not die from smoking
I have a dream
People will not make war then no one would die
I have a dream
People will not die because of drink or drugs
Because drugs do not exist.

Kaleigh Jade Lewis (11)
Hartridge High School, Newport

I Have A Dream

In my dream world
There is no racism because everyone is the same
In my dream world
There is no smoking because it is a bad example to children
In my dream world
There is no cruelty to animals
In my dream world
There is no bullying because everyone is treated the same
In my dream world
There is no drugs or alcohol abuse
As people get drunk and do stupid things
In my dream world
There is no terrorism because blowing things up is wrong
In my dream world
There is no rape because it is wrong
Men and women get along
In my dream world
There is no abuse because it is wrong
In my dream world
There is no war because we all get on with each other.

Jordan Cook (12)
Hartridge High School, Newport

I Have A Dream

To stop the war,
Let's love and care for them all,
Dropping bombs and shooting guns,
We know war isn't fun.

Evacuating children
To a different country
Let them live
With their own families.

Don't let them die,
Protect this place,
Dusty streets
And broken walls.

Oh, what is this for?
Stop this war,
Let's live in peace,
All of us happy, at least.

Sophie Mansfield (12)
Hartridge High School, Newport

Stop People Being Killed

I have a dream
That one day the Prime Minister
Will change and stop the wars
Stop people being killed
For no reason
I have a dream
The world will be a better place.

Ieuan Bufton (12)
Hartridge High School, Newport

I Have A Dream

I have a dream
For no more wars
For us all to be friends
No more fighting, no more killing
No more wars, no more wars.

I have a dream
For child abuse to end
Stop hitting the children or soon they will die
So put down the fists and all the belts
Love your children and don't abuse them.

I have a dream
For drugs to stop
Don't buy them and don't take them
Chuck them in the bin
Stop all the drugs.

I have a dream
For the litter to go
So no more on the road
Put the litter in the bin and not on the floor
So the litter must go, not stay.

I have a dream
For the world to be at peace
Let's make this world a better place.

Bethan Price (11)
Hartridge High School, Newport

My Dream

My dream is for the world to be perfect
For the world to be a better place
My dream is for no murders or wars
For no fighting and drugs
My dream is for no racism or name-calling or killing
My dream is for the world to be perfect
For the world to be a better place
Make this dream come true!

Charlene Ralph (11)
Hartridge High School, Newport

I Have A Dream

I have a dream
Some people get to live out their dreams
Why can't all people work together
And all people be forever?
Why can't all people be treated the same?
So don't be cruel and play the game
Please stop
I have a dream.

Ryan Dicks (12)
Hartridge High School, Newport

I Have A Dream!

I have a dream to stop sexual attacks
No one gets hurt or murdered
Let them be free and don't be scared.

I have a dream to stop racism
Black and white can be treated the same
They can be friends and can be equal.

I have a dream to stop all the violence
We should all get along and sing a song
We should be together without fighting
Let's keep the world at peace.

Please come true!

Libby Roberts (11)
Hartridge High School, Newport

I Have A Dream

All bullying is wrong
You've just got to be strong
Have a bit of sympathy
But it's not going to be easy.

Don't be a fool
Drugs are not cool
Not everyone has to do the same
But there's always someone else to blame.

I have a dream
But not everything is as it seems.

Thomas Marshall (12)
Hartridge High School, Newport

I Have A Dream

I have a dream
That people would stop taking drugs.

If people stopped taking drugs
They would have a good life.

Stop drugs, smoking and drinking please
Your life will be much better.

Hayley Bowyer (11)
Hartridge High School, Newport

I Have A Dream

I have a dream
For people to stop smoking and stealing
If people stop taking drugs
They will be healthier and have a better future.

I have a dream
For people to stop violence
Stop the world having wars.

I have a dream
For people to stop drinking alcohol and smoking
They will have a much better life.

Katie Marshall (12)
Hartridge High School, Newport

Have A Dream

i have a dream
War in the world stops
People are dying, our soldiers are getting killed
Think about it, just make up and go home
Go and see your family and your friends
Get rid of everything that hurts people.

So drop the guns and ditch the bombs
Then just shake hands and pray
Go see your family and be safe today.

War is wrong because people get hurt
And worried, so please . . .
Stop war!

Jessica Prothero (12)
Hartridge High School, Newport

I Have A Dream

I have a dream to make things different
To get rid of some things,
To change some things,
To make the Earth a better place.
There would be no drugs,
Or awful thugs,
No alcohol or smoking
And no, I am not joking.
The world would be a better place,
People would get along more!

Rachel Spruce (11)
Hartridge High School, Newport

Poverty

I have a dream to stop all poverty,
Don't waste food,
Some people would die for the food you waste.

Think of others instead of just yourself,
Be grateful for the food and drink that you take for granted,
Donate food that you don't want to someone in need of it.

Give to those less fortunate,
Don't buy things if you don't need them,
Buy them when you do need them.

Go to these countries less fortunate,
Then you can see how they live, to how you live,
See how they live in hunger.

It's upsetting for us to learn about it,
Imagine trying to live like it,
Think! Give to others in need!

Natalie Bevan (12)
Hartridge High School, Newport

Cruelty To Animals!

Animals should live life to the full
It's wrong if they don't
Hunters should stop hunting
It's wrong if they don't.

Why should hunters kill animals?
They don't kill us
Animals haven't done anything wrong
To deserve the cruelty they go through.

Why do some people throw out their pets
When they get old?
Why do people starve their pets
For no reason at all?

Animals have a right to live
They should live in peace
Just like everybody else in the world!

Jade Clarke (12)
Hartridge High School, Newport

I Have A Dream

I have a dream of no war
I have a dream of no poverty
I have a dream of no disasters
I have a dream of no diseases

I have a dream of no death
I have a dream of no racism
I have a dream of no cruelty to animals
I have a dream of no terrorism

I have a dream of peace
I have a dream of nobody starving
I have a dream of a world without disease
I have a dream of everyone being healthy

I have a dream of everyone living, never dying
I have a dream of everyone being treated the same
I have a dream of anti-terrorism . . .
Because that's what life is for
Living in peace
Not terror!

Conor Sweetingham (12)
Hartridge High School, Newport

My Dream

I have a dream where everyone looks the same
A dream of chocolate, the whole world is
To be queen of the world, where everyone bows down to me
I dream of money and lots of it
Everyone should smile all the time and never be down
All my family are together in my dream so we are all happy
My dreams are full of people because no one dies
I have my own underwater city, we swim all the time
I have my own mansion, I am rich, rich, rich
In my dream all animals can talk so everyone is happy
My dreams are from the future, I have my own hover car
I dream and wish all the time, I dream, I dream.

Elicia Colins (11)
Hartridge High School, Newport

I Have A Dream . . .

I have a dream there will
Be no bullying in the world
Nobody will get hurt
Everyone will be happy.

I have a dream there will
Be no child abuse
Every family will be happy
And never have any problems.

I have a dream there will
Be no cruelty to animals
Every animal will have a happy life
Just like a human.

Hannah Bishop (12)
Hartridge High School, Newport

Harassment

Harassment is silly, nasty and cruel,
People do it for their own amusement,
It's not funny and it's not nice,
You put people under a lot of pressure.

When you're harassed, you're scared and afraid,
Whether it's sex, drugs or crime,
It's not very nice and if you don't know what to do,
Don't be afraid, you're stronger than you think.

You have the power to say *no!*
You have the power to walk away,
You have your own mind, use it well,
You have your own life, do what you want with it.

Don't be silly or foolish,
Don't do drugs, don't do crime,
Don't do anything you don't want to do,
You only have one life, use it well.

Rhiannon Tucker (11)
Hartridge High School, Newport

Drugs

Don't take drugs,
They will ruin your life,
Just trust me, it will,
You need to think,
They make you steal and rob,
But at the end,
You will go to jail
And then you'll realise
What you have done.

Chloe Jones (11)
Hartridge High School, Newport

The World!

Bullies make me angry
They make we want to cry
But when there's someone bigger
To bullies, it's bye-bye.

The child abuse on Earth
Is certainly not a dream
To hear the children crying
To hear the children scream.

Why do people take them?
They must be going mad
Crack, cocaine, ecstasy
All drugs are bad!

Chantelle Davies (11)
Hartridge High School, Newport

The World

I have a dream
That animal testing is banned
And we leave the poor animals alone in their habitats.

I have a dream
That hunting was never invented
And more animals live
And would still be alive today.

I have a dream
That alcohol was never made
So people don't come home drunk.

I have a dream
That murder never happened
And people live longer
Instead of being murdered.

Kayleigh Lewis (12)
Hartridge High School, Newport

The World

I have a dream
That child abuse could be stopped
And all children could be loved by everyone
Especially their parents.

I have a dream
That racism could be stopped
And black and white people could go anywhere and everywhere
Whenever.

I have a dream
That cruelty to animals could be stopped
And they could have good homes
And be loved and cared for.

I have a dream
That drugs could be stopped
And children could walk down the streets
Without picking up needles and killing themselves.

Darrian Summers (11)
Hartridge High School, Newport

World Peace

I have a dream of world peace,
A dream which will never come true!
Many people have dreamt of this,
But still we drift further into conflict.
We fight amongst ourselves,
Or against our 'fellow' nations,
We civilians are just mere pawns on a chessboard,
Where we are sacrificed just to gain
Power over the enemy.

War has got more advanced over the years,
But it still causes thousands of tears.
War comes in many different types,
It is all around us,
People fight a war every day,
On the streets, in school and even some 'homes'
Are a *danger zone!*

We think of war with guns and things,
But I wonder
What our children's future brings?

Rhys Evans (12)
Pen-Y-Dre High School, Merthyr Tydfil

I Have A Dream

In water words are calm
On land words are like bullets
Shooting you down

The sea is peaceful
No war, drugs or thieves
Colours of calm; blues and greens

With soundless echoes of what is above
Colours of anger, red and yellow
When mindless problems erase

With blossoming minds
And gifted spirits of the future
Ideas of what might happen

The reality that happens now
Expressions on our faces
Speak for the madness above

With time on their hands
It's now or never
For the destruction
And devastation in our land
This isn't just my dream
It's my nightmare

It's not supposed to be this way
The racket of what's today
Can be silenced tomorrow

A blockage of rocks
Seems impossible to move
We are called the United Kingdom

So let us unite
Then those rocks
Will turn to pebbles . . .

Danielle Sullivan (13)
Pen-Y-Dre High School, Merthyr Tydfil

I Have A Dream

War. It's all around us.
Never since the dawn of time,
Has the world been at total peace.
When people think of war,
They tend to think of guns and bullets,
They never think of the war being fought right outside.
In our school, in our streets, in our houses,
Be it bullying, racism, murder or just petty crimes.
Millions of pounds and dollars go towards wars,
Wars with no reasons.
Wars where the people that give their lives for their countries,
Didn't even know what they were fighting for.
You can't throw money at bullying or racism to make it better,
But people could turn their attention to the real war.
Sadly, it's a losing war,
But it's the real war.

Rhys Davies (13)
Pen-Y-Dre High School, Merthyr Tydfil

I Have A Dream

I can't really change the world
I can only live it
I'm all for peace and stuff like that
But what I want is to just be me
Be with friends and have a laugh
When I'm older to just have a job
Maybe if I have a family
To go home and be with them
If my friends are still known
Go out with them and still have a laugh
So really I just want a normal life
But if I did have the power to help
Those powers wouldn't be wasted
But as I said
I can't really change the world
I can only live it.

Ryan Phillips (12)
Pen-Y-Dre High School, Merthyr Tydfil

I Have A Dream

Disaster on planet Earth
Lots of people make it worse,
Standing watching people fight,
I think that's an awful sight.

Lying in my lovely warm bed
Thinking of what the news reporter said,
Trying to think of happy thoughts
But I can't, there are people with no coats.

People on street corners all alone,
I feel like offering them a home,
Life should be a happy place,
But some people think it's a disgrace.

Standing away from all of this,
Holding onto my little sis.

Tyler Burnell (13)
Pen-Y-Dre High School, Merthyr Tydfil

I Have A Dream

As the night-time passes by,
As mist drives high,
My parents and friends,
Come out to play and watch me,
Use up my life and new ones appear.

As all little ones lose little toys,
As girls go out to chase handsome boys,
To the day as I called an angel to be my mom,
Flowers and buds come out to blossom
As friends come out to share their lost ones
To bring up new ones to watch upon us.

As devils and angels say their prayers
That's the answer to my prayer.

Tara Sullivan (12)
Pen-Y-Dre High School, Merthyr Tydfil

I Have A Dream

To care for another is a great challenge
But to care for others is an even bigger one!

My love for you will never end,
It grows and grows,
I can't pretend.

The joy you brought,
Or that's what I thought,
Will always be a great memory.

The times we had,
The times we spent,
In time my heart will mend!

Ria Lester (13)
Pen-Y-Dre High School, Merthyr Tydfil

I Have A Dream

You came into my life not so long ago
And I want you to know that I will miss you so,
You mean more to me than just a friend, a pal and a buddy,
You're the person I turn to when my life goes cruddy,
Now that the year is coming to an end,
I hope that our friendship will never bend,
Like I said, I'll miss you so
And I'll never let the memories of our friendship go.

Jade Louise Jones (13)
Pen-Y-Dre High School, Merthyr Tydfil

Love

Love is like a butterfly
Beautiful but rare
Fragile but strong
We take it for granted
And then it's gone

It comes and goes
And for the time it's here
Maybe a second, minute or day
It comes filled with brightness
But hardly ever stays

It starts small and then it grows
How it happens, nobody knows
It might make you smile
But it will always make you cry

If you manage to catch it
Hold it and hold it tight
Treasure it with your heart and soul
And don't ever let it go

Just as you think it is here to stay
You use it and abuse it
Then it flies away.

Leah Jade Roberts (13)
Pen-Y-Dre High School, Merthyr Tydfil

Poverty

I have a dream
That poverty will end
No one will suffer
Everyone will live a happy life
No worries about death
No worries about AIDS
Everyone will work together
Like a family, a happy family
Money comes together
In peace and harmony
Bob Geldof is the person who started this
We should follow in his footsteps
Keep people from the light
And give them the help they need
So Bob Geldof could use our help to pursue his dreams
To give people who suffer from poverty
The golden gift of life
If we believe
We can achieve
Together forever
I have a dream
Poverty has ended.

Zoe Phillips (13)
Pen-Y-Dre High School, Merthyr Tydfil

Be-You

Life's like a roller coaster with its ups and downs
One day it's smiles, the next it's frowns,
Never knowing what it will bring
Makes it such a wonderful thing.

Without it we wouldn't be here at all
To sample its pleasures, big or small,
Its fears and sorrows
Anger and hate
Love and passion
Ain't life great?

Kayleigh Marie Griffiths (13)
Pen-Y-Dre High School, Merthyr Tydfil

War, Poverty, Bullying And Race

People live in constant terror,
All because of human error,
It started as a silly war,
What on earth did it start for?
Some are full of anger and rage
Innocent people are locked in a cage,
People are bullied because of race,
One of the things we all have to face,
People are dying,
Their relatives are crying,
Some go out and attack,
Those just because they are black,
More will die with no aid,
Their hopes and dreams slowly fade,
No matter the colour, black or white,
Together we can put up a fight,
Dying of AIDS and starvation,
Caused by so much devastation,
They live in absolute silence,
Reliving all the violence,
Bullied because of the colour of their skin,
Tormenting their next of kin,
Victims are giving up without a fight,
Slowly going out of sight,
I have a dream,
We come together and be a team.

Gemma Meek (13)
Pen-Y-Dre High School, Merthyr Tydfil

At The End Of The Day

The destruction of Man,
took more than one life-span.
It's leading to the destruction of the Earth,
but all Man's concerned about, is how much it's worth.

We don't care what
we burn into the air.
We don't fret about where
the world's resources went.

When this Earth is gone,
we'll have nowhere else to live.
But all we're concerned about,
is the money we pay with.

At the end of the day,
we'll have no say.
At the end of the day,
we're going to pay.

Rebekah Elisabeth Ann Hughes (12)
Pen-Y-Dre High School, Merthyr Tydfil

Good Sense, Bad Sense

Imagine no ears;
No nagging, no crying, no shouting
No squawking, no screaming, no grinding
No whistling fireworks . . .

> But how I'd miss
> Laughter, chatting, my dog's bark
> Chickens chopsing
> A tuned engine, song, cheering
> And waterfalls

Imagine no eyes;
No nasty people, no slithering snakes
No ugly monster, squashed badgers or scampering spiders . . .

> But how I'd miss
> Coloured flowers, reflections,
> Computer games, Dad's face
> And budgie's feathers

Imagine no hands;
No hitting, no thumping, no writing
No peeling potatoes, no bad touching . . .

> But how I'd miss
> Stroking my cat, holding hands,
> Cuddly toys, furry carpets,
> Throwing and catching
> And hugging

Imagine no tongue;
No black coffee, no sour apples,
No disgusting medicine,
No peas or bitter orange juice
No cherries, no chilli, no sprouts . . .

> But how I'd miss
> Dolly mixtures, cakes, roast beef,
> Minty toothpaste, whiskey
> And chocolate milkshake

Imagine no nose;
No doggy smells or stinky puddles,
No sweaty armpits or sick . . .

But how I'd miss
Scented flowers, Mum's cooking
Girl's perfumes and baking bread.

Secondary English Group (14-16)
Ysgol Cedewain, Newtown

A Boy

Look at that boy asleep,
He is as a feather,
Resting peacefully on a summer day.
His breathing is as that of a river flow
But who would think:
'Tis a boy who had no
Mother,
To show him, teach him love!
'Tis a boy who all his life had
To run, hide, in torment of that
Beast that people call 'man'
Or that monstrous creature
That is 'man's' injustice.
Why doesn't He, who moulded us
Rescue us?
Some say, 'God has his ways'.
I say he acts in numerous ways
To serve our deepest desire
So you, He overlooks us.
Hear my prayer, look at that boy,
Grant him that thing that he hears of is
'Peace'.
So that, those slight seconds of rest
Be his life.
Boy don't worry. He shall
Take under His bright, blessed wings.
You shall fly, higher than any bird.
Oh, you shall ride, higher than any man
Has ever been.

Steve Uwampamo Rubayika (18)
Ysgol Uwchradd Tregaron, Ceredigion

I Have A Dream

I have a dream
Everyone can become friends
If black or white

I have a dream
That the poor
Can become rich and warm

I have a dream
That people will recycle
It saves the trees
The environment and the world

I have a dream
That the rain will go away
And the sun will come out
Every morning, 365 days a year

I have a dream
That everyone can live in peace

I have a dream
That the bullying will stop
The pain of the victims will go away

I have a dream
People all over the world
Will look before crossing the road

I have a dream
Everyone is healthy and safe.

Christina Ryan (12)
Ysgol Uwchradd Tregaron, Ceredigion

I Have A Dream Of Life

I have a dream that I can awake in the morning
And not have the need to cry.
I have a dream that I can look out of my window
And not see the years flying by.

People dying,
Blood has been lost,
Being black or white,
That is the cost.

Cancer, racism, bullying, death,
Poverty among us,
Who is going to be left?

All addicted to power,
Craving the rush,
Waiting to hear sadness,
Don't care who they push.

I have a dream that all this
Gun crime, poverty, terrorism,
Arguing, hatred and lying
Shall stop!

Ffiôn Thomas (13)
Ysgol Uwchradd Tregaron, Ceredigion

I Have A Dream

I have a dream
Our life would be
So different
From this reality

Time goes by
So slowly
Black and white
Fight, lonely

Their dream
Fell apart,
Like shattered glass
On the floor

Love is pure
And we're sure
That life is better
Than before

It's about time
For black and white
To be treated right
And equal.

Sioned & Gethin Davies (13)
Ysgol Uwchradd Tregaron, Ceredigion

The Dream

I went to bed nice and early,
My mother kissed me goodnight,
The light went off and I went to sleep
In the darkness of my room

I stood up straight out of bed
Saw all the toys on the floor
The cat was dancing and the teddy was eating
The robot was walking and Super Ted was flying

The room was alive, the toy box empty
The cowboy shooting and the Indian hiding
I jumped from my bed and joined in
Oh, this was fun, much better than sleeping!

I played the guitar for kitty to dance
And the computer had the CD on
For us all to dance and jump
And sing like the famous Madonna

The alarm went off
I jumped from my bed
Where was I? Where were the toys?
Was it all a dream? Well, a very good dream!

Rhian Lewis (14)
Ysgol Uwchradd Tregaron, Ceredigion

I Have A Dream!

I have a dream
That all children
Will be safe in their
Own homes

I have a dream
That all black and white people
Can hold hands and be a family
Friends and lovers

I have a dream
That druggies and alcoholics
Will come to their senses

I have a dream
That you and I
Can be free!

Katie Birch (13)
Ysgol Uwchradd Tregaron, Ceredigion

I Have A Dream

I have a dream
People across the land can come together
In peace and harmony

I have a dream
That young and old
Can come together without worries and fears

I have a dream
Different colours of the skin
Come as one, united through the nation

I have a dream
That rich and poor
Share and help each other
Through this tough world.

Bronwyn Coltman (13)
Ysgol Uwchradd Tregaron, Ceredigion

I Have A Dream

I have a dream
To ride a speedway bike
Round a track of dirt

I have a dream
To whizz through
The air like a hawk

I have a dream
To ride for
Wolverhampton

I have a dream
To fly like a bird

I have a dream
To be the best rider
In the world.

Daniel Bailey (13)
Ysgol Uwchradd Tregaron, Ceredigion

I Have A Dream

I have a dream that racism will end
That all black and white people will come together
And all religious people will respect people of other religions
And not fight over their own.

I have a dream
That small children will be free from abuse
That they will not get attacked by their parents
That they will get all the help and justice.

I have a dream
That all mankind will live in peace
And not be judged by their skin.

I have a dream
That all men will be created equally
Like all others, we are people
Who have feelings too.

I have a dream
That everybody will be safe and free.

Bethan Davies (13)
Ysgol Uwchradd Tregaron, Ceredigion

I Have A Dream

I have a dream that the world could be
Like an old-fashioned photo
Black and white blended in
To create a beautiful picture.

I have a dream of the world
Black and white together
All living in harmony
Against each other
Never!

Jamie Isherwood (13)
Ysgol Uwchradd Tregaron, Ceredigion

I Have A Dream

I have a dream,
A very big dream,
That everybody that's mean,
Can learn to be clean.

I have a dream,
That all the hitting and beating,
Can all cease
And we all can live in peace.

I have a dream,
That old people,
Can live the same,
Not give them all the blame.

I have a dream,
That one pen and a hand
And the 'beat bullying band'
Can make a very big difference.

Mared Hopkins (12)
Ysgol Uwchradd Tregaron, Ceredigion

Dream Of Justice

You know that hole
You feel in your soul
When a friend has died
And all you've done is cried
Times it by ten
Then times it again
That's the feeling you get
When a friend's death is met
And when they've been killed
That hole can't be filled
So why should the killer get away
When that feeling is here to stay?
They should be sent down for life
To rot in prison, where misery is rife
If they get set free
They could kill you or me
I want justice to be done
To people who kill for fun
So please send these killers down
Without a shadow of a frown.

Iannah Phillips (13)
Ysgol Uwchradd Tregaron, Ceredigion

I Have A Dream

I have a dream
That one day we will live in a world without poverty,
Where the more fortunate help the less fortunate,
Where children are not dying of hunger,
Or lack of clean water
And that every child and adult has
A roof above their heads,
A school for the children,
Little things, things we take for granted!

Every school morning you may wake
And complain that you must go to school,
But don't,
Imagine having to work and when you get home,
There being no food,
No food to help your hunger,
No drink to quench your thirst
And when you're ill, no doctor to make you better.

Imagine living in fear, that your parents
Will die of a terrible disease
And you will be left to find food for your siblings
And the fear of dying yourself.

You can make a change to this!

Aithne Baker (12)
Ysgol Uwchradd Tregaron, Ceredigion

Have A Dream

I have a dream,
That some day I'm bored,
I start to cry,
But I have nowhere to hide.

I have a dream,
That some people wish to die,
'Why, oh why?' I cry.

So many people have different lives,
Some worse, some better,
But we all deserve to live.

I have a dream,
That I was asking all the people,
'Why is life so upsetting?'

I have a dream,
That people get hurt,
They are hungry, tired and cold.

Some people think life is easy,
But it is like a roller coaster,
Up and down, you're happy, then sad.

I have a dream,
That the world is coming to an end,
Because of people committing suicide.

But I also have a dream,
That if people changed their lives,
The world would have changed too.

Vicky Hussey (12)
Ysgol Uwchradd Tregaron, Ceredigion

I Have A Dream Of Unity

Terrorism is everywhere,
Nobody seems to care,
Bombs let off lethal gases,
Killing hundreds in their masses,
Friends and relatives gone without a trace,
They might not have seen the killer's face,
Innocent people killed each day,
Without having their own say,
We're killing the world, don't you see?
We should all stand in unity.

Catherine Jones (13)
Ysgol Uwchradd Tregaron, Ceredigion

I Have A Dream

I have a dream where the sun shines strong
And all mankind lives happily for long.

I have a dream of peace and love
And words are spread by a sweet white dove.

I have a dream with no more hate,
But I am afraid it is too late.

For this dream is far from reality
And to make this work,
We should give more
To charity.

And always have love for each other,
Like an undying love for a mother.

Stop the fighting, stop the hate,
Let's stop all this on one date.

Today!

Joe Regan (13)
Ysgol Uwchradd Tregaron, Ceredigion